FRENCH SECURITY POLICY IN TRANSITION:
Dynamics of Continuity and Change

ROBBIN LAIRD

McNair Paper 38
March 1995

INSTITUTE FOR NATIONAL STRATEGIC STUDIES

NATIONAL DEFENSE UNIVERSITY
Washington, DC

INSS publishes McNair Papers to provoke thought and inform discussion on issues of U.S. national security in the post–Cold War era. These monographs present current topics related to national security strategy and policy, defense resource management, international affairs, civil-military relations, military technology, and joint, combined, and coalition operations.

Contents

FRENCH SECURITY POLICY IN TRANSITION:
Dynamics of Continuity and Change

INTRODUCTION

Since 1989, French defense and security policy has been undercut by changes in the external environment and domestic pressures to deal with the challenge of economic modernization. The Soviet revolution of 1989, the reunification of Germany, the collapse of the Soviet Union, and the experience of coalition warfare during the Gulf War—all have challenged the assumptions and realities underlying the Gaullist synthesis. Above all, the French position on security independence has been put into question. The main hope has been for a European Alliance to supplant the American one over time in the face of a gradual process of change within Europe—but change has not been gradual within Europe. The European Union is challenged by discontent within Western Europe. A new Central Europe has emerged that has yet to find its place in European or global politics. A new Russia is emergent in which nationalism is defining an assertive role for the Russians within Europe, but at the same time the economic weakness of Russia limits its ability to play such a role.

Notably, the election of President Clinton has added another challenge. The French have grown used to an assertive American role within Europe and have defined their role in part as counterbalancing the challenge of the United States. Although this definition of the French role persists (the French press's treatment of the GATT debate is typical of this definition of the French role), many senior French government officials are more concerned about the withdrawal of the United States from active engagement within Europe than with the mindless

1

countermanding of U.S. influence. For example, during a 1993 year end TV retrospective, General Moriollon was interviewed by a French journalist who asserted the following: "Isn't the US trying to assert its leadership through the UN?" Moriollon said, "No. The United States is reluctant to participate within UN missions and is very reluctant to become engaged in Bosnia." Clearly the young French journalist was shocked with this realistic response. Moriollon added: "I have just returned from the United States and know what I am talking about."

In response to the changing environment, the Balladur Government has promoted a de facto policy of transition in French foreign and security policy. But the transition has been only partial in nature: the Balladur government is a cohabitation government. Power is shared between the President and the Prime Minister in the actual conduct of foreign and security policy. In addition, the Balladur government is itself a coalition among right and center right parties. There is no clear consensus on the definition of a new French synthesis of foreign and security policy. Perhaps the election of the new President of the République in 1995 will lead to an explicit redefinition of the Gaullist synthesis or its replacement by something new.

1.
THE FRAMEWORK OF FRENCH DEFENSE AND SECURITY POLICY

The classic Gaullist synthesis of French defense and security policy emphasized four priorities:
- French independence of action
- French nuclear deterrence to protect French territory and freedom of action
- French participation in the Atlantic Alliance but not within the integrated military command
- French military intervention and arms sales to promote French interests in the Middle East and Francophone Africa.

This synthesis rested in turn on several fundamental realities:
- The United States was committed to the deterrence of Soviet expansionism and saw permanent military presence within Western Europe as a means to do so.
- There was a Soviet Union over which the Communist Party leadership exercised control of an empire.
- Germany was divided between East and West.

French European policy focused upon reconciliation with Germany and building of a European Union of like-minded West European states. French Atlantic policy sought to influence the United States by pursuing an "independent" course within the Alliance. This meant case-by-case support or criticism of the United States. But the existence of the Soviet threat ensured that the United States would stay in Europe to counter that threat regardless of French diplomatic maneuvers or actions. French détente policy toward the Soviet Union permitted France to define an "independent" course within Europe to counter the West Germans and the Americans in their own relations with the Soviet Union. French African policy permitted France to pursue

3

a policy of "grandeur" within francophone Africa that gave France the sense that it was itself more than a mere regional power and, indeed, would come to be virtually the only West European state that saw itself with global political-military missions. Finally, French policy toward the Arab world, notably in the 1970s, permitted France to expand its military arms base by becoming a major supplier in the region. It also allowed France to act as a counterweight to some extent to the United States and the Soviet Union in the region as well.

2.
KEY PUBLIC ATTITUDES
UNDERLYING
THE DEFENSE SYNTHESIS

Underlying the Gaullist defense synthesis have been persistent French public attitudes supporting a policy of national independence. There are five essential characteristics of French public support for France's independent defense policy.[1]

• First, the French continue to see defense as a requirement for public support and have continued to sense a need for a relatively high level of defense expenditure (figure 1).

• Second, the French public supports a policy of active engagement by French forces. The public supports the use of force as a tool of state power and the defense of national interests (figure 2).

• Third, the French public sees France's defense policy as being Alliance-centered. The only real debate is over whether it should be more European or Atlantic in orientation (figure 3).

• Fourth, the French public believes overwhelmingly that nuclear weapons are a necessary component in French defense policy (figure 4).

• Fifth, nuclear weapons remain a strongly supported element in the French consensus, but there is a strong belief they do not protect against all types of aggression that France is likely to encounter. In other words, there is a growing realization that nuclear weapons provide for only a partial defense of French interests (figure 5).

---

[1] All the polls in this section are taken from French MoD data as of fall 1993.

Figure 1. *Would you like the defense budget to. . .*

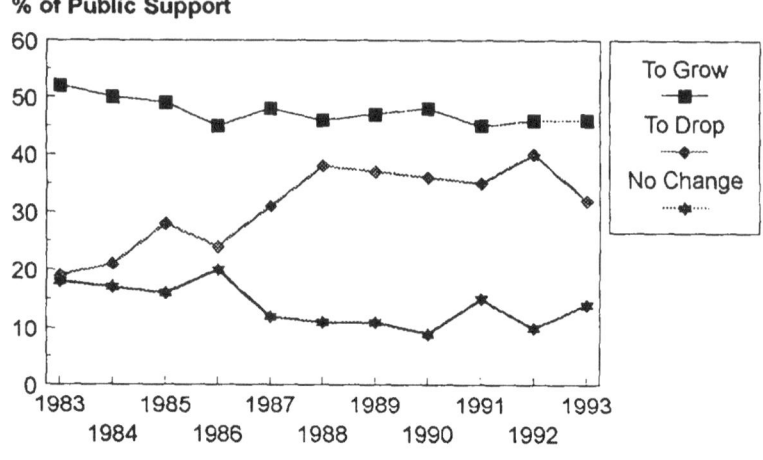

Figure 2. *Would support the use of French forces for the following reasons. . .*

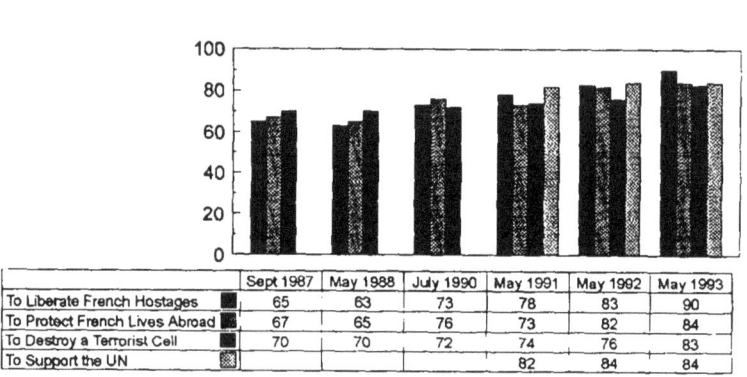

	Sept 1987	May 1988	July 1990	May 1991	May 1992	May 1993
To Liberate French Hostages	65	63	73	78	83	90
To Protect French Lives Abroad	67	65	76	73	82	84
To Destroy a Terrorist Cell	70	70	72	74	76	83
To Support the UN				82	84	84

Figure 3. *Which alliances are most useful to preserve our national security?*

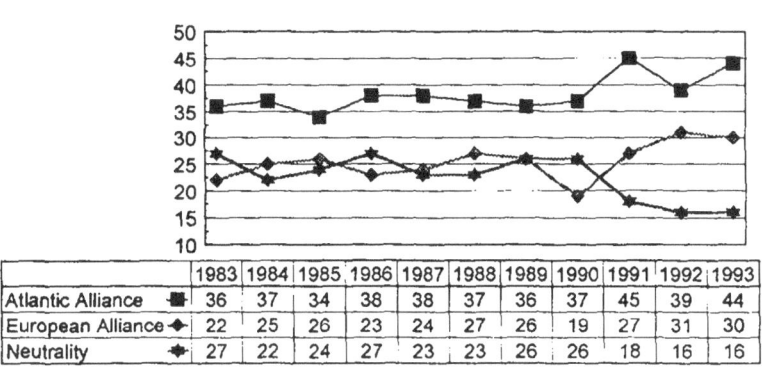

		1983	1984	1985	1986	1987	1988	1989	1990	1991	1992	1993
Atlantic Alliance	▣	36	37	34	38	38	37	36	37	45	39	44
European Alliance	◆	22	25	26	23	24	27	26	19	27	31	30
Neutrality	✦	27	22	24	27	23	23	26	26	18	16	16

Figure 4. *The role of nuclear weapons in French national defense*

% of Support in Public Opinion

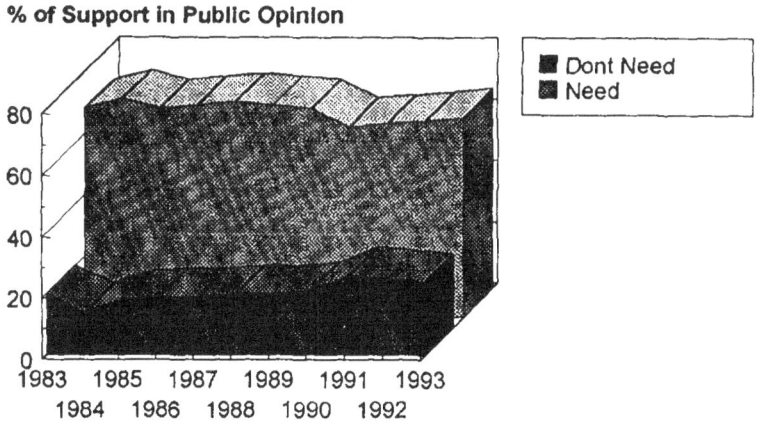

■ Dont Need
▨ Need

Figure 5. *Do nuclear weapons protect against aggression?*

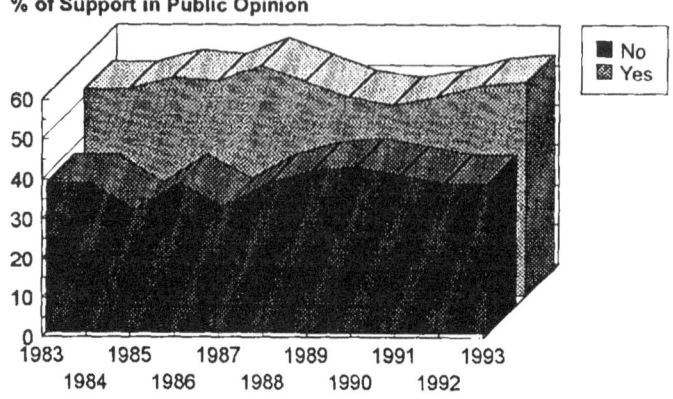

3.
THE NEW STRATEGIC ENVIRONMENT

CHALLENGES TO THE FRENCH FRAMEWORK

The Soviet revolution of 1989, the reunification of Germany, the dissolution of the Soviet Union and the Gulf War all led to a serious alteration of the reality upon which the Gaullist synthesis was built. Not surprisingly, reality has changed more rapidly than recognition that the Gaullist assumptions and approaches do not fit easily into the new post Cold War world.

The unification of Germany happened more quickly than most observers expected. With the emergence of the new Germany, the French had to adjust their policy and sort out their instincts toward the building of a common policy with the new Germany. For the French, the Germans are central to the former's defining of their own role within Europe.

The French must deal with a new Germany. Would the new Germany be a partner with France as the old West Germany had been? Was there a psychology of national renewal that would lead to German national egoism and an inability to work psychologically with the other Europeans? Or would the new Germany define its role in a more adversarial manner? Would it seek to become an overtly national competitor with France? Would such nationalism, torpedo the West European construction process?

Soon after the new Germany emerged, the Soviet Union collapsed. There was a close connection between the two processes. The Soviet Union was an empire directed from Moscow. With the collapse of communism in Germany, the weakness of the Soviet system became exposed.   Gorbachev assumed that Soviet communism could be reformed from within. He miscalculated.   Soviet communism rested upon the maintenance of empire.   Its collapse was linked to the pulling apart of the empire by the elimination of Berlin as the Western capital of Soviet communism.

The collapse of the Soviet Union and the emergence of a new Germany reopened the European question.   Eastern Europe disappeared; Central Europe reemerged.   How would the new states of Central Europe and the former Soviet Union relate to West European and Atlantic Institutions? With the collapse of the Soviet Union what would be the role of the United States in Europe writ large?   Rather than assuming that the task was to counterbalance the United States within the Western Alliance, how could France be certain the United States would remain constructively engaged in European affairs?

As the United States embraced the new opportunities in the wake of the Revolution of 1989, the French administration worried that the Americans might leave Europe too quickly, and thereby undercut the European construction process. The United States is perceived as critical to nurturing further success in the European development process, but French policy has frequently been at odds over how best to deal with the United States and Europe simultaneously.

The Soviet upheaval challenged both France's transatlantic relationship and the approach to the West European construction process.   How would France deal with the new Germany, cope with the Americans redefining themselves and address the challenges posed by the new states of Central Europe and the former Soviet Union? The classic Gaullist approach has provided no easy answers to such core questions.

No factor has been of greater significance in pushing the French over the barrier to discuss the necessity for change than the Gulf War.   The United States led a Western and Arab coalition in the war against Iraq. This military coordination was central to success in the Gulf War and showed the importance of having exercised forces in common within the Alliance. The performance of new technologies and the new concepts of the American forces (notably air-land battle) brought home to French officials and the public that the old style of warfare was passé. It is not enough to have tanks, airplanes, and isolated pieces of military equipment; modern warfare is integrated and systems-oriented. Command, control, and communication and modern forms of intelligence are indispensable in knitting together forces to fight in a modern way. Thus, the cold war system has dissipated. The European allies of France have changed. Moreover, the dynamics of the Atlantic Alliance have changed. Threats from the East have become challenges for development. The residual military challenge remains, however, especially when coupled with new challenges from North Africa and the Middle East. In short, the new strategic environment has affected the essentials of the Gaullist synthesis in three ways:

• French independence was rooted in a specific alliance framework. The French did not have to build this alliance; it was there. Now independence is exercised by creating multilateral actions, not assuming their pre-existence within a multinational alliance.

• The value and meaning of nuclear weapons have been decisively altered by the collapse of the Soviet Union. Nuclear weapons remain important but not as a central force protecting French territory from deliberate attack by a Soviet leadership bent on geopolitical hegemony.

• French military intervention and arms sales now exist in a new peacekeeping, peace enforcement, and counter-proliferation environment. The pursuit of classic state goals becomes less clear in the new multilateral and multinational setting of the European and Mediterranean security environments.

THE PLACE OF FRANCE

Developments since 1989 have challenged France in a number of ways. The end of the Cold War has meant the end of the special role of France in the Alliance and its relationship with the Soviet Union. The reopening of the European question in very fundamental ways has called into question the key institutions shaping West European development and the special role of France in its relationship with West Germany in dominating those institutions. The collapse of the superpower competition has left the United States in a special relationship with Europe, Russia, and the world. Redefining France's and Europe's relationship with America is on the historical agenda. The rapid economic growth of the Asian tigers and the uncertain futures of China and Japan have reopened critical questions of defining Asia's relationship with Europe, in general, and France, in particular. The dynamics of change in the Mediterranean basin add challenges from the south as well as to the east of Europe. Migratory, economic, cultural, and military challenges from the South add significant dimensions to the challenge of adapting Europe—notably the Western part of Europe—to the post-Cold War world.

There is a growing literature in France dealing with the variety of challenges to the French place in the world. This debate adds up to a significant shift in French perceptions—France is increasingly viewed at best as a middle-ranking power within a continent with an uncertain future in a global economic and political system undergoing dynamic transition. How should France find its bearings in this world? How should France focus its energy upon the redefinition of the role and orientation of the key West European institutions with which France is associated?

Given the propensity of the French for broad intellectual debates, discussion at the conceptual level is not to be discounted as a political factor. Indeed, many of the tracts written by politicians in France as well as their broad public pronouncements address the French challenge in the broader context of the historic transition, rather than at a technocratic level about the transition of French foreign and security policy. There are three basic positions staked out on the broad issues of the place of France in the new period of human history which we have entered:

• There are those who argue that France has a special role to play in reshaping the Western response to the post-Cold War challenges. Because of France's strong sense of national destiny and the strength of the French state and culture, France can act more cohesively than many others in this confusing period of human history. As Alain Minc has argued, the world has shifted into a period of a "new Middle Ages" and France has special strengths that can allow it to play a key role in shaping a

Western transition.[1] But it can play this role only if significant innovation takes place in France shifting the role of the state from a tutorial to an anticipatory orientation. As Guy Sormon stated:

> More of a state of obligation than a state of intervention. In the new social contract, the state would set the obligations, as during the initial period of employment in an enterprise; it would not act as the instrument of intervention. The state would hand those functions back to private actors.[2]

• There are those who argue that France has a role only to the extent to which Western Europe has a role. To the extent to which Western Europe can shift to a more effective economy and to shape a more significant multinational capability at the European level, European interests can be articulated, projected and protected.[3]

• There are those who warn that the forces of fear and of the institutional rigidity of French institutions might reduce France's role significantly in the world. Chaos can overwhelm France and reduce it to a situation of stagnation, decline and entropy.[4]

---

[1]Alain Minc, *Le nouvear âge* (Paris: Gallimard, 1993), especially chapter 10, "La grâce française."

[2] Guy Sormon, *Le Capital, suite et fins* (Paris: Fayard, 1994), 389.

[3] One of the most articulate analysts who argues this position is Christian Saint Étienne, *L'exception française* (Paris: Armand Colin, 1992) and *L'Europe contre le capitalisme* (Paris: Armand Colin, 1993).

[4] For two treatments of this trend (who argue that the trend needs to be reversed however difficult the challenge) see Alain Duhamel, *Les peurs français* (Paris: Éditions Flammarion, 1993) and Alain Peyrefitte, *La France en désarroi: Entre les peurs et l'espoir* (Paris: Éditions de Fallois, 1992).

4.
THE CHALLENGE OF ECONOMIC MODERNIZATION: France in the New Europe

The French debate about the new Europe and the role of France is focusing increasingly upon the broad challenges of post-modernity and the evolution of the post-Cold War world upon the French model of development (especially as formulated under the Fifth Republic). In part, this is a debate about French exceptionalism. Is the French model of development in the post-war world viable? Are there unique qualities to the French way of life that will persist in the competitive world of the future global economy?

One key aspect of the debate is about the viability of French society and the French/West European approach to social protection measures in the years ahead.[1] Is French society too rigid? Is it too hierarchical? Is French society too rigid to let go of social protection measures that have been implemented to buy social peace in a conflictual society?

Certainly this debate is not new. Indeed, at least since the mid-18th century French intellectuals have been debating some variant of these fundamental questions. But this is not to

---

[1] One French analyst has argued that Western Europe faces a stark choice: either continue current social protection methods or see increasing unemployment. This choice will induce serious political conflict within the French polity. Béatrice Majnoni d'Intignano, *L Protection sociale* (Paris: Éditions de Fallois, 1993). Also, the first published group of essays by the Ecole nationale d'administration reflecting the working seminars of the school focus upon the labor market and social innovation problem. *Poliques de lutte contre le chômage et l'exclusion et mutations de l'action sociale* (Paris: La documentation Française, 1994).

minimize the significance of the current variant debate only to underline its fundamental significance. The return of fundamental historical debates is a precursor to historical change. What is new about the social debate is the question of the place of the French system within a broader global system. Judgments about the French social system are often made from a comparative societal perspective and not just a French cultural perspective. This is an important manifestation of the shift in the nature of social debate in a period of global interdependence. The media and its images are increasingly becoming a core part of reality testing in social and political debates.

One of the most significant dimensions of the debate about French society entails the question of the viability or appropriateness of the French educational system to post-modern conditions. What kind of educational training is most appropriate to the new period of economic and organizational development? How should such training be administered? To whom and in what venues?

This debate has become increasingly evident in the mass media as well. For example, in a cover story in *L'Express* the gap between educational preparation and the job market was underscored. Several graphics were presented that underlined the gap between jobs likely to be created in the next 10 years and the preparation provided by the French educational system. The author concluded that "the demand for education will probably take new forms—probably less initial education and more continuous education."[2]

An important aspect of the debate about societal development entails the question of the need to cope with migratory pressures on France and Western Europe. How should France define itself in the context of the expansion of the European Union and the migration of peoples from areas south and east of Europe? What does it mean to be a citizen in the new social context? What obligations does the citizen have? What will be the role of the social protection system in dealing with migration? Will migrants gain jobs at the expense of native citizens? Will

---

[2] "Les carrières de demain: quels diplômes préparer," *L'Express*, May 5-11 1994, 127.

migrants play a positive or negative role in the redefinition of France's role in a competitive global economy?

For the French, one of the most significant debates revolves around the question of the proper role of the state in both managing a transition to a more competitive economy and in operating in a post-transition environment. What is the proper role of the state today?

It is important to note that virtually all French analysts of the dynamics of economic transition underscore the need to maintain a key role for the state, but there is a strong sense among reformers of the need to change dramatically the role of the state. As the analysts of the major reassessment to date of the role of the state in France said, "It is necessary to conceive and to flush out the reality of a state of the new type, adapted to the new economic and social age as well as relevant to the organization of the new Europe."[3]

The key judgment of most analysts of the renovation of the French state is the need to shift the state from an excessively interventionist and tutorial role to one of providing for necessary adjustments of infrastructure and broad guidance of macro-economic conditions. The need is to shift the state away from the details of bureaucratic management and excessive intervention in the private sector to playing a role of the facilitator for change.

Many of the analysts of reform note that France as a medium size county with significant social division requires a strong state. As a commentator on the French assessment in *Entreprise France* noted, the French analysts in this project compared with American analysts of a similar project on the United States emphasized a much more important role for the state in the new economic environment.[4] The American model of a weak state and a strong society works relatively well for a continental empire; it would not work well for a medium-size country trying to find its way in a very fluid situation within a continent.

---

[3] Yves Cannac, *Pour un État moderne* (Paris: Plon, 1993), 18.

[4] Benjamin Coriat and Dominique Taddéi, editors, *Enterprise France* (Paris: Le Livre de Poche, 1993)

5.
THE POLITICAL CONTEXT OF THE MODERNIZATION DEBATE

How does one connect the requisites for social, economic and organizational change with political change? There is a growing literature that addresses the dynamics of change within the French electorate. The main thrust of this analysis is to underscore the growing disaffection of the French electorate with traditional French political institutions, but there is a remaining attachment to the constitution of the Fifth Republic.[1]

The growing shifts in French public opinion provided the basis for a potential shift in the French party system and structures. For example, in an August 1994 issue of *Le Point* a comparison was made of French voting behavior in the 1989 and 1994 elections for the European parliament. The electorate committed to "institutional France" declined from 27.8 percent to 18.6 percent and overall the willingness to protest grew. More than 50 percent of the electorate abstained, and more than two-thirds of those who did vote cast their support outside of the traditional party candidates (figure 6).

One analyst underscored that the French electorate increasingly believes that the French polity does not direct and control the economic fate of France.[2] The emergence of such a belief within the electorate provides the basis for a shift in judgment about the role of the state and its rightful functions. These shifts in public opinion, however, provide only the

---

[1]See, for example, Nonna Mayer and Pascal Perrineau, *Les comportements politiques* (Paris: Armand Colin, 1992).
[2] For one of the most insightful treatments by a well known political analyst and specialist on public opinion see Roland Cayrol, *Le grand malentendu* (Paris: Éditions du Seuil, 1994).

Figure 6. *Pattern of voting*
in 1989 and 1994 European elections

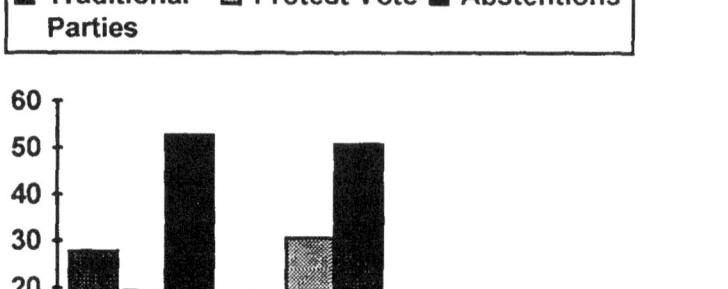

potential basis for shifts in how France is governed and how the French plutocracy operates.[3]   Current political trends indicate there are four broad alternatives emerging in the French political modernization debate.[4]

•   Rejection of France's "overemphasis" upon the need to compete in the world at large. Here an emphasis is placed on French values and the French way of life. Closing the doors to immigration and a rejection of European integration are key issues in defining this French position. The state would play a

---

[3] François Bazin and Joseph Macé-Scaron, *Le Politocrates: Vie, moeurs et coutumes de la classe politique* (Paris: Éditions du Seuil, 1993).

[4] One of the paradoxes of the dynamics of political change in France revolves around the potential significance of one of the key institutions of the Fifth Republic—the presidency—as a force for change. As Jean-Marie Colombani has noted, there is a key French paradox. "To lead a process of political recomposition as well as to respond to the need for change, for flexibility and permanent renewal of the society in front the political system, one must call upon the institution which symbolizes and incarnates the rigidity of the system itself—the président of the République. It is he which could provoke the political changes at the time of his election and which can afterwards organize the changes or consolidate rigidities." Jean-Marie Colombani, *La France sans Mitterrand* (Paris, Flammarion, 1992), 231.

key role in guiding a paternalistic reaction to the pressures from global interdependence.

• Emphasize a key role for the state in guiding France forward into a new and more competitive situation. Here the key tension would be between the paternalistic role of the state in guiding reform and the need to reduce the stranglehold which Paris and the national state have upon French society.[5]

• Emphasize incremental reform of the role of the state and its management of social and economic change. Gradually, the role of the state would be diminished vis-a-vis the society and economy. But there would be no decisive effort to draw upon political forces to reconstruct the political system to change decisively how the French economy and society operates.[6]

• Emphasize the need to reconstruct in a fundamental way the operation of French society and the economy. Here the disaffection of the French public with French institutions would be drawn upon in an effort to reconstruct the political system. A new political center would be created by drawing upon disaffected members of the left and the right. A socially responsible state would remain but the level of intervention in the economy and society would be drastically reduced.

It is difficult to understate the significance of the next presidential election and the follow-on effects of a new administration. As Cayrol argued, "In our system of politics the election of the president is a key passage point where the problems of political leadership become focused and where the political alliances of the next few years are designed and affirmed in response to the needs, fears and hopes of the French."[7]

---

[5] There are left-wing and right-wing versions of this. For an expression of the left-wing version, see André Gauran, *Chômage demande traitement de choc* (Paris: Éditions Balland, 1994). Gauran was a special advisor to then Prime Minister Bérégovoy. For a right-wing version of the paternalistic state seeking to reform society, see Jacques Chirac, *Une nouvelle France: Réflexions 1* (Paris: Nil Editions, 1994)

[6] I would generally place both Balladur and Delors in this political tendency, but both have proclivities for the second tendency as well. I would argue that Balladur but perhaps even more Delors have the potential to play the role which Colombani identified above for the new President.

[7] Roland Cayrol, *Le grand malentendu* (Paris, Éditions du Seuil, 1994), 184.

6.
FRAMING A POLICY OF TRANSITION:
The Balladur Government

The Balladur Government represents the second period of cohabitation in the Mitterrand Presidency, at period that has been very different than the first one. The Conservatives were governing in transition with a clear sense that they would win the Presidency in the 1995 election.

Unlike the first cohabitation, President Mitterrand would clearly not run again. Also, the Socialist Party was ripped by scandals and badly defeated in the elections to the National Assembly. Nonetheless, the President remained the head of the French state and the figure formally in charge of French foreign and security policy.

The Balladur government has come to power in a very challenging time for any French government. Economic difficulties abound; political limits are real. The Prime Minister is more aware than many in the French political class of the nature of the profound changes in the world forcing a rethinking of France's role in the world and its sense of itself. The main focus of his government is first survival politically and then transformation of France. Balladur is well aware of the limits of cohabitation, of his governing coalition and of the dynamics of change within Europe. He approaches the question of foreign and security policy from the standpoint of changing French domestic politics. In particular, security policy is not given a special priority by Balladur but is part of the context of a broader rethinking and reorientation of France's role in the world.

For Balladur, France must think of itself as a medium-size power; the illusion of grandeur must be avoided, and France must also more realistic about its objectives within the West. Balladur has often been quite critical of French ideologues who speak of European integration as a cure-all for French development. He issuspicious of any integration, European or NATO, that would lead to false identities. He is a convinced European, but not a European ideologue. He believes that France must find its identity within a Europe that becomes enlarged. He sees the task as one of developing several associations of states within Europe which combine into a future European Community. He has been insistent that France takes more seriously the need to include the East within the European Community as a project for European construction. There will be, inevitably, different speeds and different levels of European interaction, but he does not see this as reaching a crescendo in any point soon in some comprehensive superstate. Indeed, he is very critical of such an objective.

During his participation in the European Community (EC) summits, the Prime Minister has underscored the need for reform of the Community. He has argued for a shift in the balance of power between the Commission and the Council of Ministers. The Council as a representative of the governments of the member states must play a much greater role. The GATT dispute has accentuated the French debate about EC institutional reform. Many French critics of GATT have focused their fire on the role of the Commission in conducting negotiations without regard for the "real interests" of key member states, like France and Germany.

In part, Balladur's objection to the European ideal of the socialists is that it is utterly unrealistic. He often makes the point that France should be more flexible, as Germany has been in the past. Germany has policies toward Russia, the United States, and France. It does not confuse a European priority with France with the need to have a comprehensive East-West policy. France must become more realistic about the need to have more diversified relations.

Above all, this means coming to terms with the "Anglo-Saxons." With regard to the British, the European views of Major and Balladur are not all that far apart. Unfortunately for Balladur, the weakness of Major undercuts his ability to serve as a useful ally for dealing with the Germans and the East. The United States is viewed by Balladur to be an important player in affecting the French future. France is too weak to deal with the Americans alone; hence a European collusion is critical for France. But the Americans are critical allies for France in many areas, especially in security policy. He has made the point to Chancellor Kohl that both Germany and France need a good working relationship with the United States in security and economic policy in order to protect their interests.

He clearly rejects the goal of military integration within NATO—indeed, he is not an enthusiastic supporter of even European integration, as that is normally understood. If he rejects a too binding concept of Europe, why would he accept such a concept for military integration with the United States? "The integration of the Atlantic Alliance was designed with American preponderance in mind. It corresponded to a past epoch. But if the Alliance is to be reorganized, the integration of military forces can be organized in the same manner as during the cold war."[1] He does however see the need to reform NATO more generally to coordinate Western actions and to prepare for greater cooperation with the East. The Spanish model for the operation of NATO is close to what he has in mind for French participation—the inclusion of the Defense Planning Group (DPC) but without military integration.

The views of the Ministry of Defense under Defense Minister Leotard are clearly oriented towards French membership in the DPC and trying to use the DPC to reshape the role of NATO as an increasingly European-oriented defense organization with strong American participation. Minister Leotard has underscored a much more active French role within NATO. As he put in a radio broadcast, "The Ministry of Defense and the General Staff will involve themselves in the military committee of NATO when actions are taken which could concern France and its military forces."[2]

Such an orientation has led to France attend its first meeting of NATO defense ministers in 28 years in September 1994.

---

[1] E. Balladur, *Dictionnaire de la réforme*, Fayard, Paris, 1992, 164.

[2] "M. Leotard envisage l'eventualite d'un retrait des casques bleus au printemps," *Le Monde*, December 21, 1993, 4. See also, "L'OTAN et la France renforcent leur action conjointe," *Le Monde*, December 16, 1993, 19.

Minister Leotard attended the 2-day meeting of NATO defense ministers held in Seville, Spain. Leotard stated publicly that France had not changed its general policy toward the NATO defense structure and had agreed to attend the Seville meeting mainly because it was to focus on Bosnia. He added that France would, in the future decide whether to attend NATO defense meetings "on a case-by-case basis," but he acknowledged that France recognized "a new willingness on the part of NATO to evolve. It is possible that tomorrow, in other situations, we will again find ourselves around the (NATO) table." [3]

By redefining NATO's mission as largely one of peacekeeping, the French can help reshape NATO. They see the United States moving in a much more flexible way as well. Senior French officials could easily embrace National Security Advisor Lake's treatment of the question of multilateralism and the national military interest. "We should act multilaterally where doing so advances our interests and we should act unilaterally when that will serve our purpose." The point is that French and American approaches in practice might dovetail more closely in the future as the U.S. rethinks its role within Europe.

But the integrated command per se is viewed as an antiquated mechanism overcome by events. According to a senior French official, "No one would use the integrated command really in Bosnia—no one suggests that the Greeks and Turks will play the key role" But the integrated command will continue to exist as a bank against which assets can be drawn on a case by case basis.

The French military perceives itself to be operating almost entirely on a multilateral basis. There is a clear acceptance of multilateral cooperation in the military sphere—its operations in the Gulf War, Cambodia, and Bosnia are all multilateral in character. These operations are, however, radically different from one another in terms of the political context and need for levels of cooperative control. The main concern the military has is

---

[3] Reuters, "France backs delay in ending Bosnia arms embargo," September 28, 1994.

about too many demands for diminishing assets.[4]

For the past government, the EC and its common defense and security policy would replace NATO during the next period of European construction. For Balladur, NATO and a clear sublimation of the WEU within NATO is necessary for the ultimate emergence of some form of association of European nation states that might emerge some day. NATO exists, NATO has worked, and NATO is capable of reform,[5] and this is where the focus of attention should be. But the Americans are perceived as naive to believe that they can radically change their presence within Europe and assert the same leadership role they conducted during the Cold War.

For Balladur, there is a privileged relationship with Germany, but it is unlikely that a Franco-German alliance will protect France's interests alone. France has three possible approaches to dealing with Germany in the future. First, there could be a continuation of European integration around a Franco-German core with much greater German role. Such an integrative process will be much less focused upon a superstate and more federal in character. Also, an expansion eastward of the Community is probably critical to such a federal solution, but the French would have to accept a more subordinate role and the Germans would have to see a continued need to have a good working relationship with France. In some ways, the manner in which the German and the French governments are dealing with the franc-mark crisis is suggestive of such an approach.

---

[4] Indeed, interviews with the French military underscores high concerned they are with the uneven conduct of U.N. operations and other specific problems of the new peacekeeping interests of France and the West.

[5] It is surely a reflection of Delors sensitivity to his political role in France that led him to note in a 1993 Brussels speech, "There is no doubt that NATO is the most effective machinery for international cooperation on defense and security in Europe. It is the ultimate insurance policy against a nuclear war or a conventional attack on the territory of its Member States. At the same time it ensures American presence in Europe and provides a forum for transatlantic dialogue on all issues affecting security in the broad sense of the term. It has an effective crisis management capability, an integrated command structure and even its own military resources, such as AWACS. It is therefore an important element of stability which its members are reluctant to abandon."

Second, German leadership in dealing with the East regardless of the expansion of the West European integration process eastward would challenge the French. A new nationalism could emerge if the French and German bargain at the core of European integration truly unraveled. The weakening of multilateral structures would result from the emergence of a German-centric Europe outside the bounds of the community. Franco-German rivalry or differentiation would emerge.

Third, if this rivalry became explicit, new power balances would be pursued. The British, and the French might seek to balance Germany. The U.S. role in balancing the German relationship with Russia might emerge as central in British and French perceptions of the need to contain German power.

Balladur is acting on the first alternative, anticipates the second, but is preparing for the third if need be. He simply does not believe in a Franco-German creation of the European state. This clearly distinguishes from his cohabitation partner, President Mitterrand.

In short, it is the mixture of EC and NATO development as well as considerations of the operations of French forces in concrete political-military situations in the future which shape Balladur's approach. First, the EC must be reformed. The role of the Council of Ministers must be expanded. Political union will be deepened by an inner core of European states, most likely France-Germany-Italy-Spain-Benelux. The process of political union will encompass greater cooperation in security and defense policy. This cooperation will lead to a Eurocorps North (Franco-German core) and Eurocorps South (France-Spain-Italy) becoming operational military arms of the European Union.

At the same time, the expansion of the political union along these lines will enhance Europe's ability to cooperate with the United States within NATO. The role of NATO will continue to be especially important in dealing with the Russian challenge and the Balladur administration is willing to cooperate with the US on a variety of Russian issues, notably on safe and secure dismantlement (SSD) and comprehensive threat reduction (CTR).

But the role of the European Union (EU) is critical as well in shaping the French relationship to Russia. How will the United States come to terms with the EU role in aid in transformation of Russia? Raymond Barre has underscored the need to have a treaty between the EU and the United States to shift the American engagement from too much emphasis upon NATO at the expense of the EU. In addition in a recent interview with former French foreign Minister Jean François-Poncet, it was underscored that increasingly the reality of NATO will be shaped by the expansion of the EU's role within European security. "The EC was the economic arm of NATO. Now NATO will become the security arm of the new US-EU relationship."

The question of enlargement is critical here as well. For the French centrists, the enlargement of EU and NATO are two components of the same effort. But the United States cannot push for NATO extension without coming to terms with the EU. Notably, the first expansion will be in 1995-1996 toward the neutrals. Conditions are being laid down in this process which will shape the inclusion of the Central European states in the future. In this process, there is resentment that the United States in discussing NATO enlargement seems to ignore the impact of this issue upon the EU enlargement issue.

For the French government, the question of NATO expansion clearly takes second place to the question of the development of the European Union and the issues of EU expansion. Given the central debate about the role of European institutions in shaping French economic and cultural development, the question of the expansion of the EU has become a debate about the future of France itself. As the contest for the presidency accelerated in the fall of 1994, the key candidates to succeed President Mitterrand staked out their positions on European development. The French public overwhelmingly rejects a federalist notion of Europe and with it the inclusion of the new European states within a federal framework.

In a series of speeches in the fall of 1994, Prime Minister Balladur staked out the position most likely to reflect French policy in the years ahead He laid out a position in favor of the moderate reform of the French state, to take place within the context of a Europe of cooperation for the willing. Balladur argued that those members of the EU ready to engage in defense and security cooperation and ready to enter a currency union should do so. Those states ready to cooperate on the various dimensions of European development should begin without regard to establishing a priori the nature of the final institutional structure of Europe. The new states of Europe could become key members of the European Union as they became economically, culturally, and politically capable of so doing. He rejected the notion that NATO membership should be held out too early and without regard to the question of the capability of these states to enhance the security of the European Union, rather than to undermine it.

The Balladur plan for European stability announced in 1993, and repeated throughout 1994, is a statement of conditions for inclusion in the evolving structures of the EU. States not already members of the EU need to address minority rights. The EU states would seek to cooperate with nonmember states to stabilize their internal developments and to assist in legal and political transitions whereby minority rights would be respected. States unwilling or unable to do so would, by their behavior, deem themselves incapable of rapid inclusion within the EU.

The Franco-German summit in fall 1994 revealed potential differences between the French and the Germans on the question of how rapid the inclusions of the new states might become. The French have insisted that some sort of balance be drawn between the expansion to the east and the challenges from the south of Europe.[6]

In short, the question of enlargement of NATO and the EU have become inextricably intertwined within the domestic debates about the future of French development itself. The diplomatic room for maneuver by the new President of France will be decisively shaped by how effectively or not France proceeds in its path of economic modernization and development. Here as in many instances of French and Western security policy, domestic and foreign policy become closely interconnected in shaping the post-Cold War structures.

---

[6] "Le sommet franco-allemand face au défi de la coordination sur l'élargissement," *Les Echos*, November 29, 1994, 8; "Paris et Bonn tentent de relancer la machine européenne," *La Tribune Desfossés*, November 30, 1994, 2-3.

7.
KEY ELEMENTS OF TRANSITION IN FRENCH SECURITY POLICY

THE NUCLEAR FORCES

The nuclear weapons issue has been altered fundamentally by the end of the East-West divide and the collapse of the Soviet Union. With a hostile empire poised to threaten Western Europe with weapons of mass destruction, the European NATO allies had little choice but to rely on the United States for a nuclear umbrella. Three basic postures were used to achieve this:

• The non-nuclear West European states who, through NATO planning mechanisms and through participation in the integrated command of NATO, sought to influence U.S. decision making in a crisis.

• The British path, whereby a special relationship between London and Washington was helped along in case of crisis by the British possessing their own nuclear weapons. The British argued that their variant of the second decisionmaking center theory was designed to persuade Soviet leaders not to assume that intimidating the Americans into nonuse would do the same for British leaders.

• The French approach, where nuclear weapons were to provide independence for Paris in a crisis and to allow the French to not be subject to an American-Soviet bargain not to use nuclear weapons and to fight a conventional war in case of a general confrontation between NATO and the Warsaw Pact. But at the end of the day, French weapons came down to acting as a trigger trying to influence American calculations about the nature of an East-West war.

With the collapse of the Soviet Union, much of the rationale of these three West European approaches has been called into question. The Soviet Union has been replaced by Russia as the nuclear state possessing the capability to destroy the West in a single thrust of mutual suicide. But Russia is not the Soviet Union. The empire has collapsed and efforts to revive remnants of the empire are not about a general East-West confrontation. The challenge is about Russian zones of influence and power—conflict and controversy can easily emerge, but the role of nuclear weapons is marginal to sorting specific efforts at influence by the Russians within Europe.

The weakness of Russia as a state has raised the question of how to influence behavior of states at Russia's periphery and how Russia ought to defend itself. Many of the answers suggested in the Russian strategic debate have revolved around the role of nuclear weapons in shaping the post-Soviet strategic agenda with Europe, Asia and the United States. This has been largely a defensive approach, not characterized by an effort to heighten the sense of nuclear threat to Western Europe.

The French situation is somewhat different than the British, but the question of the relevance of nuclear weapons and their role is at stake as well. Even though the French definition of threats and of their role in the Alliance allowed them more flexibility than the British, their approach to nuclear weapons was as wedded as the British to having a Soviet enemy and an American ally.

The key difference with the British lies largely in the French maintaining a broader array of security interests than Britain—in Africa and the Mediterranean—that can credibly be linked to a new role for nuclear weapons within the French approach. Indeed, the French are restructuring their military forces to augment their flexibility and capability in dealing with military interventions, notably under international aegis. The question now becomes, what is the role of nuclear weapons in the new situation?

If one looks at French behavior rather than conceptual reinterpretation what one finds is a clear emphasis upon the priority of conventional forces in regions of direct or vital interest to France. But what is the relationship between requirements for intervention and the threat from weapons of mass destruction, notably in the Mediterranean basin? This question is emerging as a core one for the French. But does the possession of weapons of mass destruction in the hands of future proliferators create a situation in which French nuclear weapons are more or less salient? And what kind of weapons, in what kinds of roles and missions?

What is clear to some French analysts is that the classic French doctrine about nuclear forces has little relevance in this situation. The key concern of the French policy makers who built the French nuclear program was to ensure that Europe would not become the conventional military battleground for the Soviet and American superpowers.   It was a theory of nonwar—to persuade the Soviets that nuclear weapons would inevitably be used.

This approach is not easily transferred to the new situation in the Mediterranean basin. The task in this situation is to reduce direct threats to European territory and to French vital interests by blocking proliferation and augmenting the capacity of Western forces to intervene. Rather than being able to ensure that a war would be nuclear, the task now is ensure that it would not.

How does one develop credible alternatives in dealing with proliferant states in the Mediterranean basin to persuade them from ever using their nuclear weapons against Western intervention forces? This is a question focusing upon nuclear use, not nonuse to persuade a potential belligerent state not to use its nuclear weapons. This is not classic French nuclear doctrine, and debate has already started in France about this anomaly in the French approach. Although there is a clear consensus upon the need to remain a nuclear power, there is debate about what approach France should take toward nuclear deterrence in the new post cold war system.

Several key realities shape French policy in the period ahead:

• France has reduced significantly the planned expansion of its warhead arsenal. The main modality for warhead reduction has been in the planned expansion of the SLBM inventory. In addition, the planned expansion of the tactical nuclear inventory has been deferred as well (figures 7 and 8).

Figure 7. *Projected force posture in numbers of warheads*

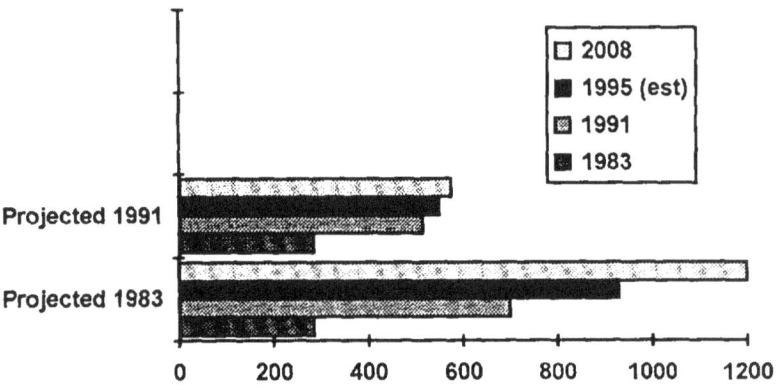

Figure 8. *1993 force structure: 651 warheads*

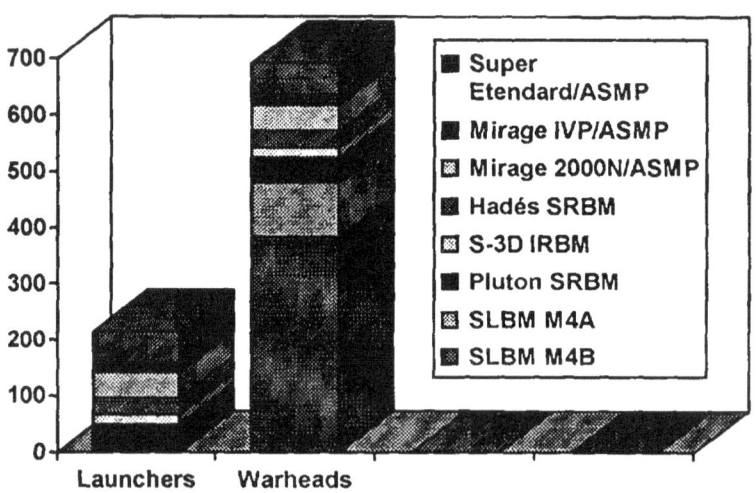

•   The French President has taken a very clear interest in pursuing a "pure" deterrence policy. The core of this policy is the notion popularized some years ago by the Chief of the Air Force General Copel that nuclear weapons only deter against nuclear attack. President Mitterrand's actions in the Gulf War were a real world test of this policy—he clearly stated that he had no intention of introducing nuclear forces into the region or into the conflict.

•   The French Government has increased the money available to the Atomic Energy Commission to maintain its testing site in the South Pacific.[1] There is a clear consensus upon the need to maintain this site for the indefinite future. The money used by the French to support their test site in French Polynesia is also a key element of maintaining French economic presence in the region and as such is seen to be useful in supporting wider goals than simply sustaining the testing program.

•   To lead to the reduced necessity for testing, France is trying to move ahead on its nuclear weapons simulation program (PALEN). But French experts have noted that several low-yield nuclear tests would be necessary to put in place the PALEN system over the next few years.

The main debate now revolves around what doctrine and force structure France needs in the period ahead. The classic French doctrine focused upon massive retaliation against the Soviet Union in a strategy of the "weak to the strong." Now the focus is upon the need to deter the "mad."[2] But how do you do this and what weapons do you need to perform this task as well?

The shift in the nuclear challenge as the French see it has been articulated quite well by Pierre Dabzies, former head of the Fondation des Etudes de Defense Nationales. "The truth is that

---

[1] Overall, the Atomic Energy Commission received a 5.9 percent increase in credits in 1994 compared to 1993. This compares with the 1992 budgetary reductions of 4.1 percent in program authorizations and 5.7 percent reductions in payment credits. The 1992 budget reduced the military-applications section of the CEA by 9.5 percent. The center-right government has thus reduced the previous government's decisions in this area.

[2] For example, see "La force de frappe veut garder ses ailes," *Liberation*, October 20, 1983, 11.

there is a key problem of the lack of adaptability of the current force structure developed against the USSR to new situations. These weapons are too powerful to make their use credible. The forces must be adapted to build less powerful arms of high energy to adapt to the new situation." [3]

There are three basic alternative scenarios for the development of the French nuclear system in the future. The first is to maintain the current force structure and levels for the indefinite future. Modernization would occur, but the land-based force at the Albion Plateau would be abandoned. The SLBM force would be modernized progressively to the M45 and then the M5 and the air component would be modernized with the acquisition of an air-launched missile of double the range of the current ASMP (air-sol moyenne portée, 100-300 kilometer range). The second alternative is to reduce the nuclear arsenal (to the sea-based component) and to develop powerful "smart" conventional weapons do carry out some current nuclear missions.   To develop this capability requires international cooperation. The third alternative would be to adapt the nuclear force to the new geostrategic context. This would require the acquisition of counter-force weapons of the most modern type in order to dissuade the new potential aggressors which would join the nuclear club.

The main weapon system involved in the debate about deterrence of the "mad" is the tactical nuclear system.[4]   Does France need an longer-range air-launched system in the future to threaten third world nuclear states? Does counter-proliferation policy for France require the acquisition of nuclear systems with a specific counter-military role?

The French White Paper released in spring 1994 articulated the nuclear challenge in the new situation as follows:

---

[3] Pierre Dabezies, *Défense Nationale*, December 1993, 55.

[4] The French Air Force Chief of Staff has argued that "The airborne missile has the most advantages in terms of versatility, flexibility and precision" and strongly supports its central role as the second component of the French nuclear force structure.

The principles of nuclear deterrence will remain viable as long as the nuclear age exists. But this is not true of the approach to fulfilling it or to the force posture itself. The force postures must always be capable of fulfilling two functions: To inflict a strike delivering unacceptable damage to the adversary and be capable of delivering a second strike; To provide for a limited strike on military targets in conformity with the last warning doctrine. The credibility of our nuclear deterrent posture lies in the possession of means sufficiently flexible and diversified to provide a range of differentiated options to the head of state when the time comes. The nuclear arsenal must be able to adapt to the evolving international situation, notably to the state of the adversaries defenses. With regard the principle of sufficiency, the number of submarines at sea will be correlated with the level of threat as well.

THE PROLIFERATION CHALLENGE

There is no strong French tradition of thinking about proliferation as a key problem for French diplomatic or defense efforts. Indeed, for a considerable period of time some French analysts considered the possibility of proliferation—albeit within limits—to be a useful instrument to stabilize global politics.[5] Furthermore, France avoided the diplomatic entrapment of arms control negotiations for a long time. Arms control was seen to be an instrument of superpower control over France that was to be contained as threat and not embraced as an opportunity.[6]

It is only very recently that some literature on proliferation has begun to appear in French. Two recent additions are a book by a French expert on the United States and on export control policy[7] and a comprehensive atlas by two prominent French

---

[5] See, for example, a French work that suggests the centrality of many of the ideas of Walzer within the French strategic identity by Michel Manel, *L'Europe face aux SS20* (Paris: Berger-Levrault, 1983).

[6] See my essay with Dinah Louda on French arms control policy in Robbin Laird, ed., *West European Arms Control Policy* (Durham, NC: Duke University Press, 1990).

[7] Marie-Hélène Labbé, *La prolifération nucléaire en 50 questions* (Paris: Jacques Bertoin, 1992)

geostrategists on the global nuclear situation.[8]

President Mitterrand began to shift French policy in the wake of the revolution of 1989. He called for a comprehensive effort of the four nuclear powers to work together to deal with the new situation created by the unification of Germany. The President continues to think in terms of how the four nuclear powers might work together in the post-Cold War period, notably on nuclear issues.

The coming of the Gulf War posed a direct threat to France. The general challenge of proliferation was raised by the Iraqi invasion of Kuwait and the response of the American-led coalition against Iraq. President Mitterrand directly rejected the use of French nuclear weapons in this theater of operations. His action poses a continuing challenge to those who think it desirable to have an effective nuclear threat to potential proliferators in the Mediterranean basin.[9]

Furthermore, Mitterrand has endorsed French participation in the Nonproliferation Treaty largely on the grounds of trying to build a comprehensive diplomatic solution to problems posed by nuclear proliferation. But the French are only in the early throes of sorting out diplomatic responses. The illness of the President and the coming French elections will almost certainly defer any dramatic shift in French policy to seek diplomatic solutions to the nuclear proliferation problem.

At the same time, there is growing awareness of the need to deal with the problem of nuclear proliferation. The French White Paper focused much of its attention on the new strategic environment upon the challenge of dealing with proliferation of weapons of mass destruction. According to the White Paper,

---

[8] Gérard Chaliand and Michel Jan, *Atlas du nucléaire: Civil et militaire* (Paris: Payot, 1993).

[9] There is also a growing ecological awareness in France that suggests the need to deal with proliferation in the Mediterranean basin. As a Mediterranean power, France is directly affected by the pollution in the region. How does a nuclear response make any sense ecologically? In other words, there is a growing possibility that ecological versus strategic consciousness will become more significant in shaping French policy on the issue of proliferation, at least in the Mediterranean basin.

"La protection" is a dimension of French strategy which also requires modernization. The protection of national territory and its approaches is a permanent mission of the national forces and a constant objective of our defense policy. The proliferation of arms of mass destruction (nuclear, biological and chemical) associated or not with ballistic missiles, will pose a new problem to our defense apparatus. This problem is posed both for the defense of our territory and for those French forces deployed abroad. This challenge concerns most of the European countries and the Atlantic Alliance.

The risks generated by various forms of proliferation can not be dealt with simply by a single response. It requires a range of responses, combing measure of "prevention," international sanctions, the exercise of deterrence and finally the employment of certain means of defense properly understood.

A balance must be sought in military strategy to define a response to these new threats, between the exercise of deterrence, the actions of prevention and interdiction and possible defenses. In the area of the anti-missile struggle, the study of which concerns at this stage the capacity of air defense and detection, notably of space based detection. The development of certain systems of air defense, some of which have already begun, and of antimissile system is also studied and will be encouraged. Given the diversity of forms which these threats can take, principally by diversified launchers, missiles and especially ballistic missiles priority will be given in this domain to the study of a concept and the means for an enlarged air defense.

* * * * *

The threat of proliferation does not follow a simple geographical or political logic. It requires to be dealt with at a global level. It necessitates international cooperation. The search for agreements which are progressively more constraining at the legal level must be accompanied by agreed upon or coordinated policies. These policies can not be simply among states holding sensitive technologies but must be made between these states and those which are tempted by a proliferation policy.

Also suggestive of the new French consciousness is the

treatment of the proliferation problem in an unusual report published by the National Assembly issued before the release of the White Paper. The proliferation problem was characterized as follows:

> The relative banalization of civilian nuclear technologies and their diffusion in an increasing number of countries accompanied by the quasi-official or de facto acquisition of the know-how to produce nuclear arms by several countries (Pakistan, Israel, South Africa, Brazil, India, etc.) have been increasing for a long time the risks of proliferation. More recently, the proliferation of the ballistic means of deliver promoted in part by Chinese exports has led to the proliferation of strategic and tactical armament of uncertain quality but with a clear increase in the overall level of global destruction capacity. Some countries (North Korea, Iraq and Iran) are making an obvious effort to develop the means to master nuclear technologies. Experts also worry about Algeria which could because of its geographic proximity represent for us in the future the biggest danger.
>
> The disintegration of the USSR has substantially increased the risks for four key reasons:
> •   The independence of three nuclearized republics—Ukraine, Belarus and Kazakhstan—and the proliferation of the centers of decision making which have either already occurred or could occur in the future
> •   The absence of the reliable control of tactical nuclear arms on the territory of the ex-Soviet Union;
> •   The uncertainties that affect in the mid-term the safety of the Ukrainian strategic nuclear arsenal;
> •   The dispersion of the nuclear scientific potential of the Soviet Union due to the deterioration of economic and social conditions in Russia.
>
> The increased risks of nuclear proliferation associated with the disintegration of the former Soviet Union can not be disassociated from the risks of ballistic missile proliferation. . . . As far as tactical nuclear arms goes, the experts are alarmed by the conditions in which some nuclear weapons are kept, particularly artillery shells whose appearance is similar to a conventional one. President Boris Yeltsin has promised to destroy these shells, but these shells have not been identified or controlled specifically and their operational use can not be prohibited by the operation of an elaborate technical code for control.

The progress made in scientific, technological and economic fields is such that the prices of less sophisticated technologies to produce nuclear weapons has decreased in a significant way. Thus, an increasing number of poor and unstable countries could acquire such weapons. Possession of such weapons is only part of the story; the threat is that "strong" belligerent governments in the Third World would stockpile such weapons and threaten their use in an irresponsible manner.

Furthermore, the same reasoning applies to the proliferation of low and high-technology conventional weapons. The reduction of military budgets in the developed world can only pressure defense industrialists to be less cautious in selling their arms. Recent conflicts (Lebanon, ex-Yugoslavia, etc.) has shown the prevalence of modern weapons and their destructive quality.

The protection which highly sophisticated systems (anti-missile, satellites, warning and detection systems) can provide against the threat of ballistic missile or chemical aggression is limited. Specialists underscore the prohibitive costs of defensive systems and their ability to provide for only limited protection. For example, the United States has reduced in a substantial way their hopes in this field. Defensive systems would not only hurt the credibility of nuclear deterrence but would also not be able to defend against all types of aggressions coming from every part of the world. They would not be able to protect against nuclear or chemical terrorism as well.

Nonetheless, one should not panic in recognizing these threats. These risks exist largely today as risks and assumptions, but one should not underestimate them. Nor should one neglect the means to prevent them militarily if the measures taken at the diplomatic and scientific level were to fail.[10]

CONVENTIONAL FORCES, MULTILATERALISM, AND PEACEKEEPING

Nuclear forces remain critical to French thinking about the new

---

[10] Arthur Paecht and Patrick Blakany, coordinators, *Rapport d'Information sur la politique militaire de la France et son financement* (Paris: The National Assembly, July 1993), 21-23.

security situation, but increasingly the role of conventional forces has been elevated to the primary place in the French approach to defense and security policy. For Prime Minister Balladur, French conventional forces are understood to be key elements of the diplomatic coinage which France has available to it to exercise influence in the new Europe. Also, Balladur has underscored that military power—notably conventional military power—is a normal power instrument for Europe in the construction of a common identity.[11]

For the Balladur administration, there has been a clear emphasis upon the new context within which French conventional forces are operating. As such, the administration has made it clear that the enhancement of the mobility of French forces and their ability to operate in multilateral settings are the core objectives of the rethinking of the role of conventional forces.

The White Paper

The French White Paper underscored the changes in the following language:

> A true conversion must gradually be carried out in the role of conventional weapons. From now on, it is their use outside the nuclear context properly speaking that prevails, even if it is necessary, especially at the beginning of the next century, to foresee possible situations where we would contribute to multinational interventions in crises involving either regional nuclear powers or, on a more long-term basis, the re-emergence of a major threat against Western Europe.
>
> The principle that nuclear deterrence must by no means be discarded is, of course, maintained, but it will come second to the capability of participating in the settlement of regional crises. This means that conventional facilities will henceforth be defined first of all by their aptitude as such to contribute, if necessary by force, to the prevention, limitation or settlement of regional crises or conflicts that do not involve the risk of extreme escalation. If this latter case presents itself, these very facilities will resume their traditional function in the deterrence maneuver, by giving concrete expression to our will to defend

---

[11] See the speech by Balladur before the Higher Defense School, May 10, 1994.

our vital interests and by enabling us to test the determination and the facilities of the potential aggressor.[12]

It is worth quoting the White Paper at some further length to underscore the perception of change within the Administration. This perception of change is a reflection of the newly emerging consensus within France:

> Our examination of the different contingencies requiring the use of our forces shows that in a great majority of cases, they will have to act far from our frontiers. The anticipated objective is that with the exception of those whose primary function in all circumstances is to ensure the security of the national territory and its approaches, all the forces must be able to intervene abroad, with the strength and in the time limits compatible with the nature of the crisis or conflict.
>
> Strategic mobility is then a decisive element of success. it depends on two factors: the aptitude of the forces to intervene in distant places and the availability of adequate transport.
>
> Apart from their specific operational capabilities, which would have to be examined, the aptitude of the forces to intervene in distant places will depend on their availability, their organization and the nature of the resources to bring into play in the theater of operations.
>
> Immediate availability in fact only concerns a small number of professional units destined to form the first echelon of a rapid deployment force, while the other echelons can be gradually brought into action, depending on how the situation evolves. On the whole, advance warnings and deadlines for a rise in power will be proportionate to the gravity of the crisis.
>
> The organization of the forces must be such as to make it possible to split them up into elementary cells which may be reassembled on demand, into coherent groups having all the capabilities of command, action, support and assistance required for the intervention. The principle of modularity will be the condition for the efficiency of the entire organization.

---

[12] The French White Paper (Ministry of Defense: Paris, 1994), 52.

And lastly, the resources brought into play by these rapid deployment forces must be designed with a view to distant engagements requiting air, sea, and land transport. These constraints, which are inherent in the technical specifications of the material, often lead to a compromise between speed, power and volume of the intervention, at least for the forces forming the first echelon.

The projection of power properly speaking is destined to check the escalation of a conflict by producing an immediate impression of superiority rather than taking the risk of a long conventional war. The range of actions covers the immediate deployment of combat planes, missiles and land forces of the first echelon up to the subsequent dispatch of reinforcements, including heavy equipment.

The NATO Context

The effort to reframe the role of French conventional forces has led to change in the assessment of the political context within which French forces are to operate. As mentioned above, French forces operate increasingly almost entirely within international settings and are seen as needing to be organized to initiate as well as blend with other states in pursuing international actions.

The Bosnian conflict has had an important impact on French thinking about the framework for the use of their conventional forces. The sense that there is a near term alternative to NATO has disappeared among key French governmental officials. Typical of the position of French center right is the report by the French national assembly cited earlier. In this report, the coordinators of this report made a number of key points concerning the situation facing French forces today and the relationship with NATO:

> The question of France's military alliances, which was frozen between 1966 and 1990, needs a substantial debate and the quick definition of a new orientation, given the multiplication of conflicts in Europe and the obvious necessity to build a European defense instrument, in particular in the context of the very long term US withdrawal.
>
> The question is not to debate about the usefulness of American presence in Europe, but to avoid too rapid a US disengagement.

It is by being present within NATO that France's opinion can be heard and the concrete experience of Yugoslavia shows that there is no credible alternative to NATO.[13]

In their recent recent article on French policy toward NATO, Johnsen and Young also underscored the nature of change in France's relation to NATO in reflecting the changing role of French conventional forces:

> The French have recognized that the dramatic changes in the European security environment have made NATO more important, not less so as they originally perceived. . . . This particularly may be the case in peace operations, which appears to be the most likely venue for the employment of French forces for the foreseeable future. Consequently, the French have insisted on increasing the power and importance of the Military Committee in Article IV missions, at the expense of Major NATO Commands. This has resulted in the Chief of the French Military Mission to the Military Committee attending as a participant, vice as an observer, for the first time since 1966 when France left the integrated command structure.... Just as the French military have returned to high level defense discussions in NATO, so, too, the French military now participate in a standing multinational structure in peacetime.[14]

Johnsen and Young added that new initiatives on the French part indicate the extent of change in French policy toward the Alliance and how the French seek to reorganize the role of conventional forces within the Alliance:

> The first example concerns command and control of the EUROCORPS. The EUROCORPS was a joint initiative of President Mitterrand and German Federal Chancellor Helmut Kohl that emerged from the Franco-German Summit at La

---

[13] Arthur Paecht and Patrick Blakany, coordinators, *Rapport d'Information sur la politique militaire de la France et son financement* (Paris: The National Assembly, July 1993).

[14] William T. Johnsen and Thomas-Durell Young, *French Policy Toward NATO: Enhance Selectivity, Vice Rapprochement* (Carlisle Barracks, PA: U.S. Army War College, September 1994), 10.

Rochelle in fall 1991. As proposed, the EUROCORPS would be based on the existing Franco-German brigade and provide the foundation for a European Defense and Security Identity. Although the Bush administration and others in the Alliance strenuously opposed the initiative as another French assault on NATO, the Germans touted the EUROCORPS as a means of easing French participation in Alliance military structures. The German view appeared vindicated when, according to press reports, on January 21, 1993, an agreement signed by the Chief of Staff of the Bundeswehr, General Klaus Naumann; then-SACEUR, General John Shalikashvili; and Admiral Lanxade placed the EUROCORPS under the operational command (vice control) of the SACEUR for the conduct of NATO missions. Thus, not only are French forces assigned to the EUROCORPS anchored within a multinational structure, but French forces could fall under the command of the SACEUR for wartime operations should nations so decide, with all the peacetime implications this implies.

The issues of NATO command and control and French forces in Article IV missions continued their evolution when, at the January 1994 NATO Summit, France agreed to U.S. initiatives for Partnership for Peace (PFP) and Combined/Joint Task Force (C/JTF). While Paris agreed, in principle, to both concepts, implementation of the initiatives has not been without expressions of French reluctance. For example, within PFP, Paris insisted that the Planning Coordination Cell (the nerve center of PFP) could not be under control of SACEUR at SHAPE, but only located at "Mons" and answerable to the North Atlantic Council in Brussels. Additionally, Paris manifested its long-held suspicions of the SACEUR during discussions concerning the development of the terms of reference for C/JTF.[15]

Key Dimensions of Change

Not only has the perceived context changed, but the French are focusing upon how to enhance the real capabilities of French forces within that context as well. The Balladur government has reversed a downward slide in French defense spending. The administration is trying to hold the line of defense spending in

---

[15] Ibid., 10-11.

the context of a vigorous national debate about economic modernization. This will be difficult to sustain over time.

Within the defense effort, the administration has focused upon priority areas to enhance the mobility and flexibility of French conventional forces. There is a renewed emphasis upon the use of military space assets to coordinate forces. There is an emphasis upon the need to make all of French conventional forces more capable of joint operations over longer distances. Indeed, it is striking how each of the services—not unlike the United States—is staking out its priority role within the mobility and power projection mission.

In addition to rethinking, the French are clearly acting within an international context to shape diplomatic outcomes. The French have provided the most soldiers to the U.N. force in Bosnia. Their experience in Bosnia has led to a close working relationship with the British. During the Cold War, the French had a close working relationship with the German Army given the sector they operated in West Germany, but had much less contact with the British. In Bosnia, the two armies have worked closely together within the context of the UN along the lines of many NATO approaches to joint operations.[16]

The French have also acted in Rwanda. Indeed, here the French led U.S. action, not the other way around. Foreign Minister Juppé clearly had in mind the use of French forces trying to trigger U.S. actions. Interviews with senior French officials during the preparation phase for the use of French forces clearly underscored concern that the military had with the context within which they would be used. The military insisted that the intervention be clearly defined and actions taken to ensure that French forces could be protected from attack by indigenous forces.

As a result of their actions rather than mere conceptualization, the French have become leaders in the process of rethinking the nature of the role of conventional forces in the new international context. For the longer term, the French are interested in peacekeeping as a means of building a European

---

[16] See for example, Xavier Gautier, *Morillon et les casques bleus: Une mission impossible?* (Paris: Edition 1, 1993).

defense identity. There is a strongly developed sense in France that enhancing European cooperation is critical to protecting France's interests in the decade ahead.

At the same time, there are two significant historical legacies shaping the immediate approach of France to peacekeeping. The first is Algeria. The divisive impact of the Algerian war on France means that there is little desire to participate in peacekeeping operations that drag France into a prolonged military operation. Similar to the American preoccupation with Vietnam, the French are shaped decisively by Algeria. The second legacy is the long-standing French experience with military intervention in Africa. The French are experienced in rapid intervention to shape political events within Africa and have built forces and operational capabilities to do this very well.

The French approach to military power is to combine a strong sense of legitimacy in the use of power for limited objects with a need to split that power between serving the interests of continental and maritime defense. Like the British, the French focus upon their maritime interests, to the South and East primarily. Like the Germans, the French focus upon their continental security interests as well. But unlike either the British or the Germans, the French try to combine both interests in a single military policy.

The role of peacekeeping for the French is to try to augment the ability of Europe to act to defend its own interests. The French have limited intervention forces to offer to this effort, but do have forces well trained in low-intensity combat operations. At the same time, the relationship with the United States remains critical to anything larger than low-intensity operations of a relatively short duration.

Another factor contributing to French rethinking about the role of their conventional forces is consideration of the future of the French defense industries. Rather than merely asserting a nation-centric approach to French defense industry, there is a clear recognition that it can survive only if it works in a broader European context.[17]   In a report for the French planning

---

[17] See, for example, "Armement: le Livre blanc prône des concentrations européennes," *Les Echos*, February 24, 1994, 8-9.

commissioned published in late 1993, it was concluded that French independence can be met only in the defense industrial area by operating in a European context.[18]   Henri Conze, director of the French defense procurement agency, has underscored that the French are seeking to accelerate European defense cooperation.   France intends to use its concurrent presidencies of the European Union and the West European Union Armaments Group (WEAG) toward that end.   French officials intend also to launch projects within the WEAG in such areas as pooling research resources and assets, introducing competition between existing test bed facilities, carrying out joint requirements studies and adopting common management methods.[19]

The French commitment to the European defense identity became especially visible in summer 1994 when the Eurocorps marched on the Champs Elysée during the July 14th national celebrations.   This was the "first time that German armor had been there since the Allied invasion of Europe ended a daily goose-step down the avenue by Adolf Hitler's Wehrmacht. '[These] are the sons of those who showed up in 1940 uninvited and shot at us,' observed Pierre Lefranc, a spokesman for veterans."[20]

In a not unrelated development, the French and German governments announced their commitment to build a joint tank for mobile operations for the Eurocorps.   At the Third International Meeting of the Ground Armaments Industries held in Paris in June 1994, the French government announced that the AMX-10 would be eventually replaced by the new joint Franco-German venture.

Although the main emphasis has been upon the need to promote European defense cooperation, there is still a key role for trans-Atlantic cooperation as well. In the areas of battlefield management and in developing joint counter-proliferation capabilities, French officials have underscored the need for

---

[18] *L'avenir des industries liées á la défense* (Paris: La documentation Française, 1993).

[19] Giovanni de Briganti, "French set out to revamp European industry," *Defense News*, October 3-9, 1994, 1 and 37.

[20] "Iron Cross, Velvet Glove," *Newsweek*, July 25, 1994, 26.

cooperation between France and the United States. For example, a recent article in *Aviation Week and Space Technology* noted that "Lockheed Martin and French Matra Defense and Space officials are discussing the potential for transatlantic cooperation on multiple information systems that would make up the electronic battlefield of the future. Both French and U.S. sides view this area as one of the major new cooperative military growth areas of the late 1990s. The embryonic nature of electronic battlefield technology makes it especially attractive as a focal point for building new transatlantic cooperation."[21]

Challenges from the South

The various themes discussed throughout this paper come together in many respects in considering evolving French perspectives on challenges from the South. The dynamics of change in North Africa, notably within Algeria, pose a clear and strongly perceived challenge within France on several levels.

First, there is concern with the impact of instability in North Africa on migration within Southern Europe, notably Italy and France. Migratory pressures in the context of already high unemployment within France and Italy is an explosive political mix within Southern Europe.

Second, the Islamic challenge to the concept of the citizen within French culture is also significant. A key theme of this paper is that the French society, economy, and polity is the throes of great change. One of the most significant aspects of that change is to the classic separation of church and state enforced by the revolutionary tradition within France as well as the notion of the nature of the nation and of the citizen within a French nation. For example, if an Islamic minority claims the right to introduce a distinct set of religious values into public education, or that same set of values challenges the loyalty of the citizen to a secular state, what would be the fate of the French concept of the nation? And of the role of the state as the custodian of that concept?

Third, political instability within Algeria can see the rise of

---

[21] *Aviation Week and Space Technology*, September 26, 1994, 83.

a fundamentalist regime on the other side of the Mediterranean. Most French specialists see the fissures within Algeria and the differences between Algeria and other Islamic states to be deep and persistent. For most specialists, there is only a low probability of a generic "Islamic" threat to Europe. Rather the concern is with Algeria itself. Fissures within Algeria lead to possible migrations; migration would take the moderates away from Algeria and enhace the position of the extremists. The radicalism of the Algerian revolution might be played out again, this time by Algerian against Algerian. Such a process of conflict might lead to the ascension to power of a minority regime capable of threatening France itself over time. The French have paid special attention to the possible acquisition by such a regime of some tools associated with weapons of mass destruction. The political challenge conjoined with the weapons of mass destruction threat could create a radically new situation for France and Southern Europe vis-a-vis North Africa. But for most specialists such a threat is not an immediate one, and key government officials such as Foreign Minister Juppé would seek to pursue policies that reduce the possibility of such a worse case scenario from occurring.

The challenge from the south is also an area where the tensions between a nationalist and multilateral orientation can be seen in French policy. For the right, there are significant forces that seek to protect the nation against the cultural, political and military threat of Islam. For the supporters of the French political leader Jean-Marie Le Pen, there is a clear rejection of the integration of the Islamic minority within the French nation. For the other articulate spokesman of conservative concerns with regard to immigration and the evolution of the French nation—Philippe de Villiers—the concern is less with the rejection of Islamic minorities than a wish to seen them integrated along the classic lines of the French citizen showing obeisance to the concept of France.[22]

At the same time, for the government of France there is growing emphasis on trying to develop a multilateral European

---

[22] See, for example, "M. de Villiers tente de fédérer ses réseaux dans un même parti," *Le Monde*, November 19, 1994, 9.

role in dealing with the south. There is a desire to have a bargain with the Germans, to have the European Union expand to the East but provide significant assets to deal with migration and development to the south. There is an effort to coordinate with the Italians and the Spanish in dealing with the political-military aspects of a Southern threat. Finally, there is a continuing desire to see the U.S. Sixth Fleet remain in the Mediterranean and to build an overall Western approach in dealing with Mediterranean security issues.

8.
CONCLUSION

The French have increasingly emphasized the international aspects of their security policy. The role of national defense remains important within the French concept, but more and more the task has been seen to use national assets to influence the evolution of the European and regional security contexts.

The French expect the United States to remain a significant player in global security policy, in general, and within Europe, in particular. But there is an expectation that the U.S. role will contract over time as the United States deals with domestic challenges and proximate security challenges—e.g., Haiti (at the expense of more distant security problems) and Bosnia.

The task for France is to try to maintain means for national defense, but in such a way as to try to maximize the influence of France within Europe and the alliance and with the United States and the Mediterranean region. Given the severe limits to the resources available for French and European defense, policy has to be framed carefully and judiciously. Policy must be evolutionary, not revolutionary. Increasingly, French security policy will be framed within the context of the French debate about economic and political modernization.

Within the context of East-West confrontation associated with the Cold War, France tried to balance three priorities—nuclear deterrence for national defense, conventional forces for a contribution to the defense of NATO against the Soviet Union, and modest intervention forces for Africa and others. With the end of the Cold War and the classic East-West confrontation, French conventional forces are being reorganized to try to maximize the capability of France to influence international interventions. Nuclear forces are being drawn down, but with a continued emphasis upon the role of nuclear deterrence for the defense of France's vital interests.

Proliferation is seen as a key dynamic in reshaping the environment within which France, Europe, and the Alliance can defend Western interests in the years ahead. There is clear concern that France's ability to intervene will be radically circumscribed by the growth in the conventional military capabilities of states in Africa and the Mediterranean basin. Also, weapons of mass destruction are looming as forces augmenting threats to Europe and as barriers to intervention outside of Europe.

Given the French commitment to nuclear deterrence, the French government wishes to pursue a policy of nonproliferation that accentuates the roles and responsibilities of the five declared nuclear powers in the Nuclear Non-Proliferation Treaty (NPT). The French have difficulties with the current overemphasis (as the French see it) upon the early completition of the Comprehensive Test Ban Treaty (CTBT) at the expense of focusing upon a more comprehensive expansion of the NPT.

The United Nations Security Council is seen to play an especially important role in trying to shape the international regime(s) necessary to deal with proliferation. Indeed, a number of developments converge on providing challenges to the role of the Security Council—Bosnia, Korea, the NPT review, and Rwanda. The French see the convergence of these challenges as simultaneous challenges to the viability of the sole international organization capable of playing a global management role.

Proliferation is seen as a challenge to NATO and the development of the European component of the Alliance as well. U.S. interest in dealing with proliferation is seen as a key component of the interest of the United States in maintaining a global presence and indeed maintaining a viable global intervention capability. For the Europeans, the direct threat from the Mediterranean basin will provide a direct threat against European—not American—territory and the emergence of this threat will provide a challenge to the formation of a European response.

But the ability of France to sustain a robust foreign and security policy will depend on the ability of the new President to be elected next year to lead a process of political and economic reform. Reforms will come at the expense of money available for defense, but without a process of reform, the political viability of the national entity will be reduced and the capacity to intervene reduced in reality.

The controversy surrounding the ratification of the Maastricht Treaty and then over GATT negotiations has underscored growing splits within the French polity over approaches to national development and the relationship of the nation to European construction. Proliferation will require a policy broader than focusing upon a narrow concept of territorial defense. The fate of French participation in a general alliance/European counter-proliferation policy will be tied to the ability of the French political system to continue the evolution of public opinion and support beyond a narrow definition of national interest—to the fate of a broader European and Western system of development.

About the Author

Robbin Laird currently is working for the Institute for Defense Analysis, where he supports the work of the congressional commission on the roles and missions of the U.S. Armed Forces. In previous assignments he worked on foreign and security policy affairs. He specializes in European and Russian security issues and has authored many books and articles on this topic. Dr. Laird received his Ph.D. from Columbia University in 1974, where he also taught for a number of years.

McNair Papers

The McNair Papers are published at Fort Lesley J. McNair, home of the Institute for National Strategic Studies and the National Defense University. An Army post since 1794, the fort was given its present name in 1948 in honor of Lieutenant General Lesley James McNair. General McNair, known as "Educator of the Army" and trainer of some three million troops, was about to take command of Allied ground forces in Europe under Eisenhower, when he was killed in combat in Normandy, 25 July 1944.

The following is a complete listing of published McNair Papers. For information on availability of specific titles, contact the Circulation Manager, Publications Directorate & NDU Press, Fort Lesley J. McNair, Washington, DC 30219-6000 (telephone: commercial 202/475-1913; DSN 335-1913).

1. Joseph P. Lorenz, *Egypt and the New Arab Coalition*, February 1989.
2. John E. Endicott, *Grand Strategy and the Pacific Region*, May 1989.
3. Eugene V. Rostow, *President, Prime Minister, or Constitutional Monarch?*, October 1989.
4. Howard G. DeWolf, *SDI and Arms Control*, November 1989.
5. Martin C. Libicki, *What Makes Industries Strategic*, November 1989.
6. Melvin A. Goodman, *Gorbachev and Soviet Policy in the Third World*, February 1990.
7. John Van Oudenaren, "The Tradition of Change in Soviet Foreign Policy," and Francis Conte, "Two Schools of Soviet Diplomacy," in *Understanding Soviet Foreign Policy*, April 1990.
8. Max G. Manwaring and Court Prisk, *A Strategic View of Insurgencies: Insights from El Salvador*, May 1990.
9. Steven R. Linke, *Managing Crises in Defense Industry: The PEPCON and Avtex Cases*, June 1990.
10. Christine M. Helms, *Arabism and Islam: Stateless Nations and Nationless States*, September 1990.
11. Ralph A. Cossa, *Iran: Soviet Interests, US Concerns*, July 1990.
12. Ewan Jamieson, *Friend or Ally? A Question for New Zealand*, May 1991.
13. Richard J. Dunn III, *From Gettysburg to the Gulf and Beyond: Coping with Revolutionary Technological Change in Land Warfare*, March 1992

14. Ted Greenwood, *U.S. and NATO Force Structure and Military Operations in the Mediterranean,* June 1993.

15. Oscar W. Clyatt, Jr., *Bulgaria's Quest for Security After the Cold War,* February 1993.

16. William C. Bodie, *Moscow's "Near Abroad": Security Policy in Post-Soviet Europe,* June 1993.

17. William H. Lewis (ed.), *Military Implications of United Nations Peacekeeping Operations,* June 1993.

18. Sterling D. Sessions and Carl R. Jones, *Interoperability: A Desert Storm Case Study,* July 1993.

19. Eugene V. Rostow, *Should Article 43 of the United Nations Charter Be Raised From the Dead?* July 1993

20. William T. Johnsen and Thomas Durell-Young; Jeffrey Simon; Daniel N. Nelson; William C. Bodie, and James McCarthy, *European Security Toward the Year 2000,* August 1993.

21. Edwin R. Carlisle, ed., *Developing Battlefield Technologies in the 1990s,* August 1993.

22. Patrick Clawson, *How Has Saddam Hussein Survived? Economic Sanctions, 1990–93,* August 1993.

23. Jeffrey Simon, *Czechoslovakia's "Velvet Divorce," Visegrad Cohesion, and European Fault Lines,* October 1993.

24. Eugene V. Rostow, *The Future of Palestine,* November 1993.

25. William H. Lewis, John Mackinlay, John G. Ruggie, and Sir Brian Urquhart, *Peacekeeping: The Way Ahead?* November 1993.

26. Edward Marks and William Lewis, *Triage for Failing States,* January 1994.

27. Gregory D. Foster, *In Search of a Post-Cold War Security Structure,* February 1994.

28. Martin C. Libicki, *The Mesh and the Net: Speculations on Armed Conflict in a Time of Free Silicon,* March 1994.

29. Patrick Clawson, ed., *Iran's Strategic Intentions and Capabilities,* April 1994.

30. James W. Morrison, *Vladimir Zhirinovskiy: An Assessment of a Russian Ultra-Nationalist,* April 1994.

31. Patrick M. Cronin and Michael J. Green, *Redefining the U.S.-Japan Alliance: Tokyo's National Defense Program,* November 1994.

32. Scott W. Conrad, *Moving the Force: Desert Storm and Beyond,* December 1994.

33. John N. Petrie, *American Neutrality in the 20th Century: The Impossible Dream,* January 1995.

34. James H. Brusstar and Ellen Jones, *The Russian Military's Role in Politics*, January 1995.

35. S. Nelson Drew, *NATO from Berlin to Bosnia: Trans-Atlantic Security in Transition*, January 1995.

36. Karl W. Eikenberry, *Explaining and Influencing Chinese Arms Transfers*, February 1995.

37. William W. Mendel and David G. Bradford, *Interagency Cooperation: A Regional Model for Overseas Operations*, March 1995.

38. Robbin Laird, *French Security Policy in Transition: Dynamics of Continuity and Change*, March 1995.